Summary of

The Ideal Team Player

How to Recognize and Cultivate The Three Essential Virtues

by Patrick Lencioni

Instaread

Please Note

This is a summary with analysis.

Copyright © 2016 by Instaread. All rights reserved worldwide. No part of this publication may be reproduced or transmitted in any form without the prior written consent of the publisher.

Limit of Liability/Disclaimer of Warranty: The publisher and author make no representations or warranties with respect to the accuracy or completeness of these contents and disclaim all warranties such as warranties of fitness for a particular purpose. The author or publisher is not liable for any damages whatsoever. The fact that an individual or organization is referred to in this document as a citation or source of information does not imply that the author or publisher endorses the information that the individual or organization provided. This concise summary is unofficial and is not authorized, approved, licensed, or endorsed by the original book's author or publisher.

Table of Contents

Overview 4

Important People 7

Key Takeaways..9

Analysis 11

Key Takeaway 1 11

Key Takeaway 2 13

Key Takeaway 3 14

Key Takeaway 4 16

Key Takeaway 5 17

Key Takeaway 6 19

Key Takeaway 7 20

Key Takeaway 8 21

Key Takeaway 9 23

Author's Style 26

Author's Perspective 27

References 29

Overview

Patrick Lencioni's *The Ideal Team Player: How to Recognize and Cultivate The Three Essential Virtues* posits that in order to succeed—especially in a work environment—one must be a team player. Business leaders must be able to identify and hire team players to secure the best possible advantage over their competitors and leverage all the benefits of teamwork. Ideal team players share three core virtues: They are hungry, humble, and smart. To illustrate the ideal team player model in practice, Lencioni offers the hypothetical example of Valley Builders, a construction firm in Napa. Using this extended hypothetical as referent, Lencioni illustrates the components of the ideal team and explains how to apply them.

Valley Builders was founded some 30 years ago by Bob Shanley. On the advice of his doctor, Shanley is retiring, but at a critical juncture: the firm has just inked deals on its two biggest jobs to date. As it turns out, his nephew Jeff is more than happy to leave his consulting job in Silicon Valley and take the reins of Valley Builders from his uncle. He's rightly concerned that it's a major risk to have VB stretched to the limit with these two big projects just as he's stepping into leadership. But as Bob explains, from a cash-flow standpoint, their hands are tied; they have to complete both.

Jeff immediately turns to Bobby Brady, who runs VB's field operations, and Clare Massick, head of finance, legal, and HR. They agree that what VB needs first and foremost is more staff. In fact, they need to hire more people than the typical industry standard is for the jobs in question because turnover at VB is relatively high. Certain members of the team are less than ideal team players, which is causing truly ideal team players to leave.

Together, Jeff, Bobby, and Clare identify the key virtues of an ideal team player: hunger, humility, and people smarts. They promote, hire, and fire according to their perceptions of these qualities. Most notably, they promote to an executive position an existing employee with those three virtues after an especially promising candidate who is sorely lacking in humility withdraws his application. Meanwhile, they have a frank discussion with another team leader about how her lack of people smarts is causing friction on one of the key contract job sites. She shores up this virtue to such a degree that she becomes one of the company's most valuable employees. Within 30 days, they see marked improvements, and a year into the new hiring practices, the company is working better than ever before.

The Valley Builders fable demonstrates how having just one or two of the ideal team-player virtues is not enough; ideal team players have all three and in roughly equal measure. While each virtue has its merits, what makes them effective is how they work together to support and reinforce a culture of teamwork.

The ideal team player model can be used not just to hire new people, but to both evaluate and professionally develop existing employees. Clearly identifying and rewarding examples of the three virtues is a way to make teamwork the backbone of an organization's culture, one that is apparent not only to employees, but also to vendors, partners, and customers.

Important People

Patrick Lencioni is the author of *The Ideal Team Player* and the founder and president of The Table Group, a Bay Area management consulting firm. He is a well-known speaker on organizational management and leadership as well as the author of nine of other books, among them the bestseller *Five Dysfunctions of a Team* (2002) and *The Advantage: Why Organizational Health Trumps Everything Else in Business* (2012).

Characters from the Valley Builders fable:

Jeff Shanley co-founded a successful Silicon Valley start-up before taking over Valley Builders, his uncle's construction company.

Bob Shanley founded and ran Valley Builders for three decades before health problems forced him to step down.

Clare Massick runs the Valley Builders human resources department as well as finance and legal operations.

Bobby Brady heads up field operations at Valley Builders.

Ted Marchbanks recently retired from a larger competitor, North Bay Construction, and is being considered for a vice president of field operations position at Valley Builders, reporting to Bobby.

Nancy Morris is one of two project managers on Valley Builders' Oak Ridge shopping site contract.

Craig is the other project manager on the Oak Ridge contract, in charge of hard landscaping materials and civic infrastructure.

Key Takeaways

1. Organizations that make teamwork one of their core values must be able to identify and hire ideal team players.

2. Ideal team players have three core virtues: they are humble, hungry, and, smart.

3. Ideal team players have each of the three virtues in roughly equal measure.

4. Of the three virtues, humility is the most important.

5. People who lack humility either tend to be arrogant or fail to recognize their own self-worth.

6. Hunger is detrimental to the team when it is exclusively self-interested or when taken to an extreme.

7. Smart people don't always use their social intelligence for the benefit of the group.

8. The ideal team player criteria can first be applied within an organization when hiring new employees.

9. Criteria for the ideal team player can also be used when evaluating and developing current employees.

Instaread on The Ideal Team Player

Thank you for purchasing this Instaread book

**Download the Instaread mobile app to get
unlimited text & audio summaries
of bestselling books.**

Visit Instaread.co
to learn more.

Analysis

Key Takeaway 1

Organizations that make teamwork one of their core values must be able to identify and hire ideal team players.

Analysis

Teamwork is a core feature of the culture at Valley Builders. In fact, Bob had hired Jeff to lead a teamwork session at VB the year before he took over for his uncle. But when Bobby and Clare tell Jeff that Bob's intolerance of employees who don't mesh with the culture is one of the reasons that overall staff turnover is so high, Jeff rightly sees this as a red flag. While he doesn't doubt for a moment that former staff members didn't fit in, the onus is on Valley Builders to hire the right people in the first place. So if it's teamwork that Valley Builders values in company culture, then the company needs to be able to identify and hire team players. Yet when pressed to define "team player," the best Bobby and Clare can muster is "not a jackass."

An organization's culture is the product of various ingredients. Some are purposefully chosen, others less so. Ultimately, organizational culture is a reflection of the organization's values both in theory and in practice. Infrastructure, policies, and processes can assist in upholding or dismantling an organization's culture, as the Canadian Health Services Research Foundation discovered when interviewing providers for a report on teamwork in that country's health care industry. It found that teams in institutional health care settings, which work in the same building and are internally supported by resources and a hierarchy of management and administration, have an especially clear view of what it means to be a team member. [1] However, even the most teamwork-oriented infrastructure, policies, and processes can't overcome the attitudes and related behaviors of the employees themselves. As such, the ability to identify and hire the employees who will uphold and perpetuate an organization's chosen culture is critical.

Key Takeaway 2

Ideal team players have three core virtues: they are humble, hungry, and, smart.

Analysis

Merriam-Webster defines "team player" as "someone who cares more about helping a group or team to succeed than about his or her individual success." [2] Ostensibly, anyone can claim to feel that way. That's why Jeff sat down with Bobby and Clare to define a team player in terms of positive, demonstrated individual characteristics.

People who are humble by definition don't consider themselves to be better than other people. They do not seek to be praised for their own individual ideas or actions. Instead, they are more interested in doing great work than in receiving accolades, which is why they try to elevate the interests of the group over their own. "Hungry" describes an appetite for more: more opportunity, more responsibility, and more work. Hungry people have drive, which is why they typically need very little in the way of pushing from their managers. In the context of teammates and teamwork, "smart" describes someone who is able to work well with other people. Put another way, it's an ability to read the room. Although intelligence is obviously important for any job, knowing how to work well with others is often even more so. At Valley Builders, for example, Nancy does not have great people smarts—her way of managing the people who report to her has caused more than one employee to leave the company.

Key Takeaway 3

Ideal team players have each of the three virtues in roughly equal measure.

Analysis

It's not enough to have one or even two of these virtues and not a third; in fact, the result can be decidedly negative. Someone who is hungry and smart but who is deficient in humility, for example, is essentially a skillful politician. Ted Marchbanks says all the right things to both Jeff and Clare during his interview process. But even after having multiple interactions with Kim, an HR assistant who works at reception, he doesn't bother to learn her name. Nancy, meanwhile, who is both humble and hungry but deficient in people smarts, is an accidental irritant in the company. She doesn't mean to turn people off or cause problems, but her lack of interpersonal skills almost guarantees it.

Identifying personality types in order to improve business success became a popular pursuit in the twentieth century. The Myers-Briggs Type Indicator (MBTI) is the best known and most widely used instrument. Based on Carl Jung's theory of psychological types, it identifies four dichotomies for how people interact with the world around them: introversion vs. extroversion, sensing vs. intuition, thinking vs. feeling, and judging vs. perceiving. The Myers-Briggs questionnaire identifies 16 different personality types. [3] It is widely touted as being a useful tool for building successful teams based on the assumption that by knowing each team member's type, the team can be structured with a balance of these characteristics. If a balance is struck, the strengths and weaknesses of each team player compensate for and complement one another in the most constructive way possible.

Key Takeaway 4

Of the three virtues, humility is the most important.

Analysis

Humility is a prerequisite for the ability to put the needs of the group above those of the self. Ted Marchbanks, despite his hunger and smarts, has a notable lack of humility, and he ultimately withdraws his candidacy for the VP of field operations job. Craig, who is also hungry and smart but who is described as the opposite of a self-promoter, is given the job instead.

Humility is considered by many religions to be among the most important virtues a person can demonstrate. For example, perhaps one of the most widely recognized quotes from the New Testament is Matthew 5:5: "Blessed are the meek: for they shall inherit the earth." [4] In Judaism, Niddah 30b in the Talmud reads: "Even if the world tells you, 'You are righteous,' consider yourself a sinner." [5] These exhortations to humility have strongly shaped Western values over the course of two millennia.

Key Takeaway 5

People who lack humility either tend to be arrogant or fail to recognize their own self-worth.

Analysis

A lack of humility is generally rooted in insecurity, but it can manifest in opposite ways including arrogance. The toxic effect an arrogant team member can have on cohorts is fairly obvious because it is hardly an endearing personality trait. When Ted Marchbanks neglects to remember Kim's name, for example, he displays the arrogance that was noticed during the interview process. Shortly after he withdraws and Craig is given the position, a former colleague of Ted's confirms on no uncertain terms that he would not have been a good fit for VB.

Indeed, in some case, a colleague's arrogance can be downright dangerous. Consider the character of Major Frank Burns in the hit American TV show *M*A*S*H*. His arrogance blinds him to his own lack of skill as a surgeon, which puts the life of more than one patient on the line and negatively impacts both the effectiveness and the morale of the other doctors and nurses in the unit. While he longs to be promoted, he's similarly unskilled as a commander; each time he's temporarily put in charge, he finds a new way to place his own ego ahead of the needs of everyone else in the unit.

But not all arrogance is so obvious as that of Frank Burns. Arrogance can easily be confused with confidence, a misperception some job candidates will work to exploit during the interview process in order to get the job. Holding interviews in non-traditional settings in order to remove candidates from their comfort zone is one way to better observe their true character.

On the other end of the spectrum are people who have a very diminished sense of self, and who, as a result, question or downplay what they bring to the team. They are frustrating at best and at worst ineffective as their lack of confidence drags the rest of the team down with them. In the TV show *Parks and Recreation*, character Jerry Gergich displays a crippling lack of confidence despite his talents, which negatively impacts his work. As a result, not only does he make mistakes his colleagues are left to fix, but he is the perpetual butt of their jokes. The lack of respect his team members have for him is best exemplified by the various ways he is addressed or referred to over the show's seven seasons, from Jerry to Larry to Gary.

Key Takeaway 6

Hunger is detrimental to the team when it is exclusively self-interested or when taken to an extreme.

Analysis

In order for hunger to support teamwork, it can't be solely focused on promoting one's own self-interest. Identifying those who are only looking to further themselves can be especially challenging for hiring managers. It's difficult to know where an employee's hunger will be directed ahead of time, and few people will allow themselves to display overtly narcissistic tendencies during the interview process. When hunger is exclusively focused on the self, it's often a red flag for a lack of skill rather than an abundance of it. The character Michael Scott on the TV show *The Office* is not especially good at his job, but nevertheless constantly seeks to make everything at work about him, both within the Dunder Mifflin office environment and beyond.

Nor will hunger be additive if the work is the person's sole focus, superseding personal or community interests. Balance is necessary. Think of Tracy Flick from Alexander Payne's 1999 film *Election*. While she is clearly bright and motivated, her relentless pursuit of the student council presidency makes her an insufferable presence to everyone around her, in particular, one of her teachers, who unsuccessfully tries to derail her chances at the polls.

Key Takeaway 7

Smart people don't always use their social intelligence for the benefit of the group.

Analysis

History is littered with examples of smart people with purely evil intentions. Con artists need to be deft and intelligent to execute their schemes. Consider the example of Bernie Madoff, whose Ponzi scheme swindled billions of dollars from the clients of his prestigious financial management company. Central to executing his scam was the daily backdating of investor trades—trades that never actually took place. Not only were his investors in the dark, but Madoff's former employees alleged in court following his arrest that they were tricked into helping to facilitate the scheme on his behalf. They moreover alleged that he purposely sought out employees whose knowledge of securities was unsophisticated. [6] Madoff illustrates the dangers of having an unscrupulous, non-team-oriented person in charge of hiring.

Key Takeaway 8

The ideal team player criteria can first be applied within an organization when hiring new employees.

Analysis

Perpetuating a company's core culture is primarily achieved by identifying, hiring, and maintaining employees who support and reinforce that culture. Without the "right" people, the effect of any policies and infrastructure will be severely compromised.

Hiring the "right" people in terms of company culture is not a new idea. A 1991 study that sought to uncover how employee-organization fit is established and maintained, and to what end, confirmed that new recruits whose values match those of the company adjust to their jobs more quickly. Moreover, it found that those whose values most closely match that of the company are the most satisfied. These employees intend to stay with the company for a long time and often do. [7]

Tony Hsieh, founder and CEO of online shoe store Zappos, learned first-hand how important finding the right employees is for maintaining a successful business after the culture "went completely downhill" at his first company, LinkExchange. [8] At Zappos, the number one priority is company culture. "Our whole belief is that, if you get the culture right, most of the other stuff like delivering great customer service or building a long-term, enduring brand will just happen naturally, on its own," he told an audience at a Stanford Technology Ventures Program gathering in 2010. Getting the culture right, he notes, "starts with the hiring process." [9]

Hiring the right people from the get-go will save the most time, money, and heartache for everyone in the long run. In one international survey, whose respondents represented a mix of business functions, industries, organization sizes, and geographic locations, 59 percent said they'd rejected potential candidates based on a lack of cultural fit. [10] Interviewers should ask specific questions, sometimes more than once, and be honest about the virtues of hunger, humility, and smarts they are seeking and why they are necessary in light of the company's culture. They should be unafraid to choose cultural fit over experience. In the same survey, 78 percent said it's easier to develop job fit than it is to develop cultural fit, which likely explains why 59 percent said they'd support letting "high potential" employees go if they didn't fit with the company culture. [11]

Key Takeaway 9

Criteria for the ideal team player can also be used when evaluating and developing current employees.

Analysis

Employee assessments should be used to determine if existing staff are ideal team players and, if not, to decide whether with the company's help they can improve or would be better off elsewhere. An employee interview or self-assessment is generally a better option than peer evaluations because peer evaluations are prone to being both personal and political.

For employees who might benefit from professional development, one of three outcomes should be expected. They will act on feedback to improve; they will decide that they are not a good fit for the company and then resign; or they will appear to accept the feedback but do nothing to change, thereby forcing the company to find a replacement. It is incumbent upon the company to make its culture of teamwork clear in this way to both incoming and existing employees.

As workforces become more distributed and project-based, instilling and reinforcing company culture can seem more challenging than ever. And yet teams are more important than ever before according to a 2016 report on Global Human Capital Trends by consulting firm

Deloitte. [12] In surveying some 7,000 human resources and business practice leaders from 130 countries, the firm found that in order to become more flexible and responsive to customers' needs, organizations are revamping their organizational designs. Rather than the traditional, function-focused approach, they are building networks of project-based teams that can be assembled and dismantled according to the needs of the organization. [13] Deloitte likens this new "network of teams" model to that of Hollywood movie-making in which function-specific specialists come together for a limited period of time to produce a film. [14] While those specialists—be they actors, hair and makeup stylists, or gaffers—may belong to shared unions or have the same agents, they will go their separate ways once filming wraps with no guarantee that they will ever work together again.

Against the backdrop of this disrupted and shifting workplace landscape, company leaders must learn to recognize opportunities to reward team player behaviors and to discourage those that hamper teamwork in ways that are visible to other members of the team, not just on a one-on-one basis. Offering employees who exhibit pro-team behaviors accolades at regularly scheduled team meetings or project-focused conference calls is among the simplest and most impactful ways to reward such behavior. Discouraging behaviors that don't support the team, however, needs to be undertaken with particular care. One way is to put the feedback into the hands of the group by facilitating group sessions whereby team members identify behaviors that both support and detract from the team in the abstract without naming names. That way there is less opportunity for public shaming or singling out of certain individuals. All present are able to witness the group agreeing on which behaviors benefit the group and which ones don't.

Author's Style

Lencioni devotes approximately three-quarters of *The Ideal Team Player* to a fable that illustrates his central arguments. He then transitions to first-person narration to define the model in more explicit detail and offer tangible guidance on ways to apply it to organizations. His writing style is simple and direct, and his fable includes very little information that does not directly support his thesis. When he describes the desired traits and behaviors of an ideal team member, Lencioni's consulting background is evident. The advice he offers is practical and directed at leaders and managers of organizations, not employees. He also uses his first-person narration to explain the origins of the book as well as how it relates to his best-known title, *Five Dysfunctions of a Team* (2002), which considers the group dynamics necessary to yield successful teamwork.

Author's Perspective

Lencioni founded The Table Group, a management consulting firm based in Lafayette, California, in 1997, and continues to serve as its president. He has written nine other management and leadership books, most notably the New York Times bestseller *Five Dysfunctions of a Team* (2002). He is also a renowned keynote speaker.

Before founding The Table Group, Lencioni worked at Sybase, Oracle, and the consulting firm Bain & Co. He grew up in Bakersfield, California, and considers himself an evangelical Catholic. He points to the Bible when singling out humility as the most important of the three virtues and holds up Christ as the best example of it. While his faith is central to his family life and friendships, Lencioni believes his interactions with non-Catholic Christians have had a bigger impact on his career than his Catholicism. [15]

~~~~ **END OF INSTAREAD** ~~~~

Thank you for purchasing this Instaread book

Download the Instaread mobile app to get unlimited text & audio summaries of bestselling books.

Visit Instaread.co to learn more.

References

1. Oandasan, Ivy, et al. "Teamwork in healthcare: promoting effective teamwork in healthcare in Canada. Policy synthesis and recommendations." In *Teamwork in healthcare: promoting effective teamwork in healthcare in Canada. Policy synthesis and recommendations.* Canadian Health Services Research Foundation, 2006. p. 12. Accessed June 21, 2016. http://www.cfhi-fcass.ca/migrated/pdf/teamwork-synthesis-report_e.pdf

2. "team player." Merriam-Webster. Accessed June 13, 2016. http://www.merriam-webster.com/dictionary/team%20player

3. "MBTI Basics." The Myers & Briggs Foundation. Accessed June 9, 2016. http://www.myersbriggs.org/my-mbti-personality-type/mbti-basics/

4. Matthew 5:5. King James Bible Online. Accessed June 20, 2016. https://www.kingjamesbibleonline.org/Matthew-5-5/

5. Baron, Joseph L. *A Treasury of Jewish Quotations.* New York: J. Aronson, Inc., 1985, p. 445.

6. Larson, Erik. "Ex-Madoff Exec Tells Jury Not Fazed by Backdated Trades." *Bloomberg,* Feb. 25, 2014. Accessed June 21, 2016. http://www.bloomberg.com/news/articles/2014-02-24/

ex-madoff-employee-says-secretarial-job-was-her-only-goal

7. Chatman, Jennifer A. "Matching People and Organizations: Selection and Socialization in Public Accounting Firms." *Administrative Science Quarterly* Vol. 36, No. 3 (September 1991): 459-484. Accessed June 21, 2016. http://www.jstor.org/stable/2393204

8. Hsieh, Tony. *Delivering Happiness: A Path to Profits, Passion, and Purpose.* Grand Central Publishing, 2010, p. 134.

9. Hsieh, Tony. "Culture is Priority One - Tony Hsieh (Zappos)." Stanford Technology Ventures Program. Uploaded June 12, 2011. Accessed June 21, 2016. https://www.youtube.com/watch?v=-4D3RplqmyU

10. "Cubiks International Survey on Job Cultural Fit." Cubiks. Accessed June 10, 2016. http://admin.cubiks.com/SiteCollectionDocuments/Files%20ENG/Research%20Studies%20ENG/Cubiks%20Survey%20Results%20July%202013.pdf

11. Ibid.

12. Bersin, Josh, et al. "Global Human Capital Trends 2016: The new organization: Different by design." Deloitte Touche Tohmatsu Ltd.

p. 11. Accessed June 10, 2016. http://www2.deloitte.com/global/en/pages/human-capital/articles/introduction-human-capital-trends.html

13. Ibid.

14. Ibid.

15. Hain, Randy. "A Practicing Catholic Surrenders to Christ: An Interview with Best Selling Author Patrick Lencioni." *The Integrated Catholic Life*. May 7, 2010. Accessed June 6, 2016. http://www.integratedcatholiclife.org/2010/05/patrick-lencioni-a-practicing-catholic-surrenders-to-christ-an-interview-with-best-selling-author/

Lightning Source UK Ltd.
Milton Keynes UK
UKHW020340240819
348481UK00015B/1275/P